Shane Tadlock's
FISHERMAN'S JOURNAL

Shane Tadlock

ANDANTE PUBLISHING
REDMOND, WA

Shane Tadlock's FISHERMAN'S JOURNAL
Copyright © 2008 Shane Tadlock

Cover art by Shane Tadlock
Interior art by Shane Tadlock

Book design by Jessica W. Chandler

Printed in the United States of America

1 3 5 7 9 10 8 6 4 2

Library of Congress cataloging-in-publication data to come:
Tadlock, Shane

Shane Tadlock's FISHERMAN'S JOURNAL / Shane Tadlock

Andante Publishing
22222 Union Hill Road
Redmond, WA 98053

ISBN - 978-0-9639167-1-6

This Fisherman's Journal belongs to:

_____

If found, please return to:

_____

_____

_____

Or call:

_____

As a dedicated (some would say addicted) fisherman, I fish for many different species in many different places throughout the year (I mean, week). I grew tired of asking myself questions like: When did the steelhead start running here last year? What were we using that time on the Klickitat River when it was so high and muddy? Who was I with when we caught so many walleye out on Bank's Lake? and so on...

It was then that I came up with the idea of a fisherman's journal. I have found that documenting and reviewing my fishing adventures has increased my catch rates as well as provided me with a lot of enjoyment. My hope is that this journal will do the same for you.

Good luck out there and keep a sharp hook!

- Shane

DATE: _____

LOCATION FISHED: _____
_____
_____

WEATHER CONDITIONS: _____
_____
_____

WATER CONDITIONS: _____
_____
_____

FISH CAUGHT: _____
_____
_____

METHODS/COMMENTS: _____
_____
_____
_____
_____
_____
_____
_____

DATE: _____

LOCATION FISHED: _____
_____
_____

WEATHER CONDITIONS: _____
_____
_____

WATER CONDITIONS: _____
_____
_____

FISH CAUGHT: _____
_____
_____

METHODS/COMMENTS: _____
_____
_____
_____
_____
_____
_____
_____

DATE: _____

LOCATION FISHED: _____

_____

_____

WEATHER CONDITIONS: _____

_____

_____

WATER CONDITIONS: _____

_____

_____

FISH CAUGHT: _____

_____

_____

METHODS/COMMENTS: _____

_____

_____

_____

_____

_____

_____

_____

DATE: _____

LOCATION FISHED: _____
_____
_____

WEATHER CONDITIONS: _____
_____
_____

WATER CONDITIONS: _____
_____
_____

FISH CAUGHT: _____
_____
_____

METHODS/COMMENTS: _____
_____
_____
_____
_____
_____
_____
_____

DATE: _____

LOCATION FISHED: _____
_____
_____

WEATHER CONDITIONS: _____
_____
_____

WATER CONDITIONS: _____
_____
_____

FISH CAUGHT: _____
_____
_____

METHODS/COMMENTS: _____
_____
_____
_____
_____
_____
_____
_____

DATE: _____

LOCATION FISHED: _____
_____
_____

WEATHER CONDITIONS: _____
_____
_____

WATER CONDITIONS: _____
_____
_____

FISH CAUGHT: _____
_____
_____

METHODS/COMMENTS: _____
_____
_____
_____
_____
_____
_____
_____

10

DATE: _____

LOCATION FISHED: _____
_____
_____

WEATHER CONDITIONS: _____
_____
_____

WATER CONDITIONS: _____
_____
_____

FISH CAUGHT: _____
_____
_____

METHODS/COMMENTS: _____
_____
_____
_____
_____
_____
_____
_____

11

DATE: _____

LOCATION FISHED: _____
_____
_____

WEATHER CONDITIONS: _____
_____
_____

WATER CONDITIONS: _____
_____
_____

FISH CAUGHT: _____
_____
_____

METHODS/COMMENTS: _____
_____
_____
_____
_____
_____
_____
_____

DATE: _____

LOCATION FISHED: _____
_____
_____

WEATHER CONDITIONS: _____
_____
_____

WATER CONDITIONS: _____
_____
_____

FISH CAUGHT: _____
_____
_____

METHODS/COMMENTS: _____
_____
_____
_____
_____
_____
_____
_____

13

DATE: _____

LOCATION FISHED: _____

_____

_____

WEATHER CONDITIONS: _____

_____

_____

WATER CONDITIONS: _____

_____

_____

FISH CAUGHT: _____

_____

_____

METHODS/COMMENTS: _____

_____

_____

_____

_____

_____

_____

_____

DATE: _____

LOCATION FISHED: _____
_____
_____

WEATHER CONDITIONS: _____
_____
_____

WATER CONDITIONS: _____
_____
_____

FISH CAUGHT: _____
_____
_____

METHODS/COMMENTS: _____
_____
_____
_____
_____
_____
_____
_____

DATE: _____

LOCATION FISHED: _____

_____

_____

WEATHER CONDITIONS: _____

_____

_____

WATER CONDITIONS: _____

_____

_____

FISH CAUGHT: _____

_____

_____

METHODS/COMMENTS: _____

_____

_____

_____

_____

_____

_____

_____

DATE: _____

LOCATION FISHED: _____
_____
_____

WEATHER CONDITIONS: _____
_____
_____

WATER CONDITIONS: _____
_____
_____

FISH CAUGHT: _____
_____
_____

METHODS/COMMENTS: _____
_____
_____
_____
_____
_____
_____

17

DATE: _____

LOCATION FISHED: _____
_____
_____

WEATHER CONDITIONS: _____
_____
_____

WATER CONDITIONS: _____
_____
_____

FISH CAUGHT: _____
_____
_____

METHODS/COMMENTS: _____
_____
_____
_____
_____
_____
_____
_____

DATE: _____

LOCATION FISHED: _____
_____
_____

WEATHER CONDITIONS: _____
_____
_____

WATER CONDITIONS: _____
_____
_____

FISH CAUGHT: _____
_____
_____

METHODS/COMMENTS: _____
_____
_____
_____
_____
_____
_____

DATE: _____

LOCATION FISHED: _____
_____
_____

WEATHER CONDITIONS: _____
_____
_____

WATER CONDITIONS: _____
_____
_____

FISH CAUGHT: _____
_____
_____

METHODS/COMMENTS: _____
_____
_____
_____
_____
_____
_____
_____
_____

DATE: _____

LOCATION FISHED: _____
_____
_____

WEATHER CONDITIONS: _____
_____
_____

WATER CONDITIONS: _____
_____
_____

FISH CAUGHT: _____
_____
_____

METHODS/COMMENTS: _____
_____
_____
_____
_____
_____
_____
_____

DATE: _____

LOCATION FISHED: _____
_____
_____

WEATHER CONDITIONS: _____
_____
_____

WATER CONDITIONS: _____
_____
_____

FISH CAUGHT: _____
_____
_____

METHODS/COMMENTS: _____
_____
_____
_____
_____
_____
_____
_____

DATE: _____

LOCATION FISHED: _____
_____
_____

WEATHER CONDITIONS: _____
_____
_____

WATER CONDITIONS: _____
_____
_____

FISH CAUGHT: _____
_____
_____

METHODS/COMMENTS: _____
_____
_____
_____
_____
_____
_____
_____

DATE: _____

LOCATION FISHED: _____
_____
_____

WEATHER CONDITIONS: _____
_____
_____

WATER CONDITIONS: _____
_____

FISH CAUGHT: _____
_____
_____

METHODS/COMMENTS: _____
_____
_____
_____
_____
_____
_____
_____

DATE: _____

LOCATION FISHED: _____
_____
_____

WEATHER CONDITIONS: _____
_____
_____

WATER CONDITIONS: _____
_____
_____

FISH CAUGHT: _____
_____
_____

METHODS/COMMENTS: _____
_____
_____
_____
_____
_____
_____
_____

25

DATE: _____

LOCATION FISHED: _____
_____
_____

WEATHER CONDITIONS: _____
_____
_____

WATER CONDITIONS: _____
_____
_____

FISH CAUGHT: _____
_____
_____

METHODS/COMMENTS: _____
_____
_____
_____
_____
_____
_____
_____
_____

DATE: _____

LOCATION FISHED: _____
_____
_____

WEATHER CONDITIONS: _____
_____
_____

WATER CONDITIONS: _____
_____
_____

FISH CAUGHT: _____
_____
_____

METHODS/COMMENTS: _____
_____
_____
_____
_____
_____
_____
_____

DATE: _____

LOCATION FISHED: _____
_____
_____

WEATHER CONDITIONS: _____
_____
_____

WATER CONDITIONS: _____
_____
_____

FISH CAUGHT: _____
_____
_____

METHODS/COMMENTS: _____
_____
_____
_____
_____
_____
_____
_____

DATE: _____

LOCATION FISHED: _____
_____
_____

WEATHER CONDITIONS: _____
_____
_____

WATER CONDITIONS: _____
_____
_____

FISH CAUGHT: _____
_____
_____

METHODS/COMMENTS: _____
_____
_____
_____
_____
_____
_____
_____

DATE: _____

LOCATION FISHED: _____
_____
_____

WEATHER CONDITIONS: _____
_____
_____

WATER CONDITIONS: _____
_____
_____

FISH CAUGHT: _____
_____
_____

METHODS/COMMENTS: _____
_____
_____
_____
_____
_____
_____
_____

DATE: _____

LOCATION FISHED: _____
_____
_____

WEATHER CONDITIONS: _____
_____
_____

WATER CONDITIONS: _____
_____
_____

FISH CAUGHT: _____
_____
_____

METHODS/COMMENTS: _____
_____
_____
_____
_____
_____
_____
_____

DATE: _____

LOCATION FISHED: _____
_____
_____

WEATHER CONDITIONS: _____
_____
_____

WATER CONDITIONS: _____
_____
_____

FISH CAUGHT: _____
_____
_____

METHODS/COMMENTS: _____
_____
_____
_____
_____
_____
_____

DATE: _____

LOCATION FISHED: _____
_____
_____

WEATHER CONDITIONS: _____
_____
_____

WATER CONDITIONS: _____
_____
_____

FISH CAUGHT: _____
_____
_____

METHODS/COMMENTS: _____
_____
_____
_____
_____
_____
_____
_____

DATE: _____

LOCATION FISHED: _____
_____
_____

WEATHER CONDITIONS: _____
_____
_____

WATER CONDITIONS: _____
_____
_____

FISH CAUGHT: _____
_____
_____

METHODS/COMMENTS: _____
_____
_____
_____
_____
_____
_____
_____

DATE: _____

LOCATION FISHED: _____
_____
_____

WEATHER CONDITIONS: _____
_____
_____

WATER CONDITIONS: _____
_____
_____

FISH CAUGHT: _____
_____
_____

METHODS/COMMENTS: _____
_____
_____
_____
_____
_____
_____
_____

DATE: _____

LOCATION FISHED: _____
_____
_____

WEATHER CONDITIONS: _____
_____
_____

WATER CONDITIONS: _____
_____
_____

FISH CAUGHT: _____
_____
_____

METHODS/COMMENTS: _____
_____
_____
_____
_____
_____
_____
_____

DATE: _____

LOCATION FISHED: _____
_____
_____

WEATHER CONDITIONS: _____
_____
_____

WATER CONDITIONS: _____
_____
_____

FISH CAUGHT: _____
_____
_____

METHODS/COMMENTS: _____
_____
_____
_____
_____
_____
_____
_____

DATE: _____

LOCATION FISHED: _____
_____
_____

WEATHER CONDITIONS: _____
_____
_____

WATER CONDITIONS: _____
_____
_____

FISH CAUGHT: _____
_____
_____

METHODS/COMMENTS: _____
_____
_____
_____
_____
_____
_____
_____

DATE: _____

LOCATION FISHED: _____
_____
_____

WEATHER CONDITIONS: _____
_____
_____

WATER CONDITIONS: _____
_____
_____

FISH CAUGHT: _____
_____
_____

METHODS/COMMENTS: _____
_____
_____
_____
_____
_____
_____
_____

DATE: _____

LOCATION FISHED: _____
_____
_____

WEATHER CONDITIONS: _____
_____
_____

WATER CONDITIONS: _____
_____
_____

FISH CAUGHT: _____
_____
_____

METHODS/COMMENTS: _____
_____
_____
_____
_____
_____
_____
_____

DATE: _____

LOCATION FISHED: _____
_____
_____

WEATHER CONDITIONS: _____
_____
_____

WATER CONDITIONS: _____
_____
_____

FISH CAUGHT: _____
_____
_____

METHODS/COMMENTS: _____
_____
_____
_____
_____
_____
_____

41

DATE: _____

LOCATION FISHED: _____
_____
_____

WEATHER CONDITIONS: _____
_____
_____

WATER CONDITIONS: _____
_____
_____

FISH CAUGHT: _____
_____
_____

METHODS/COMMENTS: _____
_____
_____
_____
_____
_____
_____
_____

DATE: _____

LOCATION FISHED: _____
_____
_____

WEATHER CONDITIONS: _____
_____
_____

WATER CONDITIONS: _____
_____
_____

FISH CAUGHT: _____
_____
_____

METHODS/COMMENTS: _____
_____
_____
_____
_____
_____
_____
_____

DATE: _____

LOCATION FISHED: _____

_____

_____

WEATHER CONDITIONS: _____

_____

_____

WATER CONDITIONS: _____

_____

_____

FISH CAUGHT: _____

_____

_____

METHODS/COMMENTS: _____

_____

_____

_____

_____

_____

_____

_____

DATE: _____

LOCATION FISHED: _____
_____
_____

WEATHER CONDITIONS: _____
_____
_____

WATER CONDITIONS: _____
_____
_____

FISH CAUGHT: _____
_____
_____

METHODS/COMMENTS: _____
_____
_____
_____
_____
_____
_____

DATE: _____

LOCATION FISHED: _____

_____

_____

WEATHER CONDITIONS: _____

_____

_____

WATER CONDITIONS: _____

_____

_____

FISH CAUGHT: _____

_____

_____

METHODS/COMMENTS: _____

_____

_____

_____

_____

_____

_____

_____

DATE: _____

LOCATION FISHED: _____
_____
_____

WEATHER CONDITIONS: _____
_____
_____

WATER CONDITIONS: _____
_____
_____

FISH CAUGHT: _____
_____
_____

METHODS/COMMENTS: _____
_____
_____
_____
_____
_____
_____
_____

DATE: _____

LOCATION FISHED: _____

_____

_____

WEATHER CONDITIONS: _____

_____

_____

WATER CONDITIONS: _____

_____

_____

FISH CAUGHT: _____

_____

_____

METHODS/COMMENTS: _____

_____

_____

_____

_____

_____

_____

_____

DATE: _____

LOCATION FISHED: _____
_____
_____

WEATHER CONDITIONS: _____
_____
_____

WATER CONDITIONS: _____
_____
_____

FISH CAUGHT: _____
_____
_____

METHODS/COMMENTS: _____
_____
_____
_____
_____
_____
_____
_____

DATE: _____

LOCATION FISHED: _____
_____
_____

WEATHER CONDITIONS: _____
_____
_____

WATER CONDITIONS: _____
_____
_____

FISH CAUGHT: _____
_____
_____

METHODS/COMMENTS: _____
_____
_____
_____
_____
_____
_____

DATE: _____

LOCATION FISHED: _____
_____
_____

WEATHER CONDITIONS: _____
_____
_____

WATER CONDITIONS: _____
_____
_____

FISH CAUGHT: _____
_____
_____

METHODS/COMMENTS: _____
_____
_____
_____
_____
_____
_____

DATE: _____

LOCATION FISHED: _____
_____
_____

WEATHER CONDITIONS: _____
_____
_____

WATER CONDITIONS: _____
_____
_____

FISH CAUGHT: _____
_____
_____

METHODS/COMMENTS: _____
_____
_____
_____
_____
_____
_____
_____

DATE: _____

LOCATION FISHED: _____
_____
_____

WEATHER CONDITIONS: _____
_____
_____

WATER CONDITIONS: _____
_____
_____

FISH CAUGHT: _____
_____
_____

METHODS/COMMENTS: _____
_____
_____
_____
_____
_____
_____

DATE: _____

LOCATION FISHED: _____
_____
_____

WEATHER CONDITIONS: _____
_____
_____

WATER CONDITIONS: _____
_____
_____

FISH CAUGHT: _____
_____
_____

METHODS/COMMENTS: _____
_____
_____
_____
_____
_____
_____
_____

DATE: _____

LOCATION FISHED: _____
_____
_____

WEATHER CONDITIONS: _____
_____
_____

WATER CONDITIONS: _____
_____
_____

FISH CAUGHT: _____
_____
_____

METHODS/COMMENTS: _____
_____
_____
_____
_____
_____
_____
_____

DATE: _____

LOCATION FISHED: _____
_____
_____

WEATHER CONDITIONS: _____
_____
_____

WATER CONDITIONS: _____
_____
_____

FISH CAUGHT: _____
_____
_____

METHODS/COMMENTS: _____
_____
_____
_____
_____
_____
_____
_____

DATE: _____

LOCATION FISHED: _____
_____
_____

WEATHER CONDITIONS: _____
_____
_____

WATER CONDITIONS: _____
_____
_____

FISH CAUGHT: _____
_____
_____

METHODS/COMMENTS: _____
_____
_____
_____
_____
_____
_____
_____
_____

DATE: _____

LOCATION FISHED: _____
_____
_____

WEATHER CONDITIONS: _____
_____
_____

WATER CONDITIONS: _____
_____
_____

FISH CAUGHT: _____
_____
_____

METHODS/COMMENTS: _____
_____
_____
_____
_____
_____
_____

DATE: _____

LOCATION FISHED: _____
_____
_____

WEATHER CONDITIONS: _____
_____
_____

WATER CONDITIONS: _____
_____
_____

FISH CAUGHT: _____
_____
_____

METHODS/COMMENTS: _____
_____
_____
_____
_____
_____
_____
_____

DATE: _____

LOCATION FISHED: _____
_____
_____

WEATHER CONDITIONS: _____
_____
_____

WATER CONDITIONS: _____
_____
_____

FISH CAUGHT: _____
_____
_____

METHODS/COMMENTS: _____
_____
_____
_____
_____
_____
_____
_____

DATE: _____

LOCATION FISHED: _____
_____
_____

WEATHER CONDITIONS: _____
_____
_____

WATER CONDITIONS: _____
_____
_____

FISH CAUGHT: _____
_____
_____

METHODS/COMMENTS: _____
_____
_____
_____
_____
_____
_____
_____

DATE: _____

LOCATION FISHED: _____
_____
_____

WEATHER CONDITIONS: _____
_____
_____

WATER CONDITIONS: _____
_____
_____

FISH CAUGHT: _____
_____
_____

METHODS/COMMENTS: _____
_____
_____
_____
_____
_____
_____
_____

DATE: _____

LOCATION FISHED: _____
_____
_____

WEATHER CONDITIONS: _____
_____
_____

WATER CONDITIONS: _____
_____

FISH CAUGHT: _____
_____
_____

METHODS/COMMENTS: _____
_____
_____
_____
_____
_____
_____
_____

DATE: _____

LOCATION FISHED: _____
_____
_____

WEATHER CONDITIONS: _____
_____
_____

WATER CONDITIONS: _____
_____
_____

FISH CAUGHT: _____
_____
_____

METHODS/COMMENTS: _____
_____
_____
_____
_____
_____
_____
_____

DATE: _____

LOCATION FISHED: _____
_____
_____

WEATHER CONDITIONS: _____
_____
_____

WATER CONDITIONS: _____
_____
_____

FISH CAUGHT: _____
_____
_____

METHODS/COMMENTS: _____
_____
_____
_____
_____
_____
_____
_____

DATE: _____

LOCATION FISHED: _____

_____

_____

WEATHER CONDITIONS: _____

_____

_____

WATER CONDITIONS: _____

_____

_____

FISH CAUGHT: _____

_____

_____

METHODS/COMMENTS: _____

_____

_____

_____

_____

_____

_____

_____

DATE: _____

LOCATION FISHED: _____
_____
_____

WEATHER CONDITIONS: _____
_____
_____

WATER CONDITIONS: _____
_____
_____

FISH CAUGHT: _____
_____
_____

METHODS/COMMENTS: _____
_____
_____
_____
_____
_____
_____
_____

DATE: _____

LOCATION FISHED: _____
_____
_____

WEATHER CONDITIONS: _____
_____
_____

WATER CONDITIONS: _____
_____
_____

FISH CAUGHT: _____
_____
_____

METHODS/COMMENTS: _____
_____
_____
_____
_____
_____
_____
_____

DATE: _____

LOCATION FISHED: _____
_____
_____

WEATHER CONDITIONS: _____
_____
_____

WATER CONDITIONS: _____
_____
_____

FISH CAUGHT: _____
_____
_____

METHODS/COMMENTS: _____
_____
_____
_____
_____
_____
_____
_____

DATE: _____

LOCATION FISHED: _____
_____
_____

WEATHER CONDITIONS: _____
_____
_____

WATER CONDITIONS: _____
_____
_____

FISH CAUGHT: _____
_____
_____

METHODS/COMMENTS: _____
_____
_____
_____
_____
_____
_____

DATE: _____

LOCATION FISHED: _____
_____
_____

WEATHER CONDITIONS: _____
_____
_____

WATER CONDITIONS: _____
_____
_____

FISH CAUGHT: _____
_____
_____

METHODS/COMMENTS: _____
_____
_____
_____
_____
_____
_____

DATE: _____

LOCATION FISHED: _____
_____
_____

WEATHER CONDITIONS: _____
_____
_____

WATER CONDITIONS: _____
_____
_____

FISH CAUGHT: _____
_____
_____

METHODS/COMMENTS: _____
_____
_____
_____
_____
_____
_____
_____

DATE: _____

LOCATION FISHED: _____
_____
_____

WEATHER CONDITIONS: _____
_____
_____

WATER CONDITIONS: _____
_____
_____

FISH CAUGHT: _____
_____
_____

METHODS/COMMENTS: _____
_____
_____
_____
_____
_____
_____
_____

DATE: _____

LOCATION FISHED: _____
_____
_____

WEATHER CONDITIONS: _____
_____
_____

WATER CONDITIONS: _____
_____
_____

FISH CAUGHT: _____
_____
_____

METHODS/COMMENTS: _____
_____
_____
_____
_____
_____
_____
_____
_____

DATE: _____

LOCATION FISHED: _____
_____
_____

WEATHER CONDITIONS: _____
_____
_____

WATER CONDITIONS: _____
_____
_____

FISH CAUGHT: _____
_____
_____

METHODS/COMMENTS: _____
_____
_____
_____
_____
_____
_____
_____

DATE: _____

LOCATION FISHED: _____
_____
_____

WEATHER CONDITIONS: _____
_____
_____

WATER CONDITIONS: _____
_____
_____

FISH CAUGHT: _____
_____
_____

METHODS/COMMENTS: _____
_____
_____
_____
_____
_____
_____

DATE: _____

LOCATION FISHED: _____
_____
_____

WEATHER CONDITIONS: _____
_____
_____

WATER CONDITIONS: _____
_____
_____

FISH CAUGHT: _____
_____
_____

METHODS/COMMENTS: _____
_____
_____
_____
_____
_____
_____
_____
_____

77

DATE: _____

LOCATION FISHED: _____
_____
_____

WEATHER CONDITIONS: _____
_____
_____

WATER CONDITIONS: _____
_____
_____

FISH CAUGHT: _____
_____
_____

METHODS/COMMENTS: _____
_____
_____
_____
_____
_____
_____
_____

DATE: _____

LOCATION FISHED: _____
_____
_____

WEATHER CONDITIONS: _____
_____
_____

WATER CONDITIONS: _____
_____
_____

FISH CAUGHT: _____
_____
_____

METHODS/COMMENTS: _____
_____
_____
_____
_____
_____
_____
_____

DATE: _____

LOCATION FISHED: _____
_____
_____

WEATHER CONDITIONS: _____
_____
_____

WATER CONDITIONS: _____
_____
_____

FISH CAUGHT: _____
_____
_____

METHODS/COMMENTS: _____
_____
_____
_____
_____
_____
_____
_____

DATE: _____

LOCATION FISHED: _____
_____
_____

WEATHER CONDITIONS: _____
_____
_____

WATER CONDITIONS: _____
_____
_____

FISH CAUGHT: _____
_____
_____

METHODS/COMMENTS: _____
_____
_____
_____
_____
_____
_____
_____

DATE: _____

LOCATION FISHED: _____
_____
_____

WEATHER CONDITIONS: _____
_____
_____

WATER CONDITIONS: _____
_____
_____

FISH CAUGHT: _____
_____
_____

METHODS/COMMENTS: _____
_____
_____
_____
_____
_____
_____
_____

DATE: _____

LOCATION FISHED: _____

_____

_____

WEATHER CONDITIONS: _____

_____

_____

WATER CONDITIONS: _____

_____

_____

FISH CAUGHT: _____

_____

_____

METHODS/COMMENTS: _____

_____

_____

_____

_____

_____

_____

_____

DATE: _____

LOCATION FISHED: _____
_____
_____

WEATHER CONDITIONS: _____
_____
_____

WATER CONDITIONS: _____
_____
_____

FISH CAUGHT: _____
_____
_____

METHODS/COMMENTS: _____
_____
_____
_____
_____
_____
_____

DATE: _____

LOCATION FISHED: _____
_____
_____

WEATHER CONDITIONS: _____
_____
_____

WATER CONDITIONS: _____
_____
_____

FISH CAUGHT: _____
_____
_____

METHODS/COMMENTS: _____
_____
_____
_____
_____
_____
_____
_____

DATE: _____

LOCATION FISHED: _____
_____
_____

WEATHER CONDITIONS: _____
_____
_____

WATER CONDITIONS: _____
_____
_____

FISH CAUGHT: _____
_____
_____

METHODS/COMMENTS: _____
_____
_____
_____
_____
_____
_____
_____

DATE: _____

LOCATION FISHED: _____
_____
_____

WEATHER CONDITIONS: _____
_____
_____

WATER CONDITIONS: _____
_____
_____

FISH CAUGHT: _____
_____
_____

METHODS/COMMENTS: _____
_____
_____
_____
_____
_____
_____
_____

DATE: _____

LOCATION FISHED: _____
_____
_____

WEATHER CONDITIONS: _____
_____
_____

WATER CONDITIONS: _____
_____
_____

FISH CAUGHT: _____
_____
_____

METHODS/COMMENTS: _____
_____
_____
_____
_____
_____
_____
_____

DATE: _____

LOCATION FISHED: _____
_____
_____

WEATHER CONDITIONS: _____
_____
_____

WATER CONDITIONS: _____
_____
_____

FISH CAUGHT: _____
_____
_____

METHODS/COMMENTS: _____
_____
_____
_____
_____
_____
_____
_____

DATE: _____

LOCATION FISHED: _____
_____
_____

WEATHER CONDITIONS: _____
_____
_____

WATER CONDITIONS: _____
_____
_____

FISH CAUGHT: _____
_____
_____

METHODS/COMMENTS: _____
_____
_____
_____
_____
_____
_____
_____

DATE: _____

LOCATION FISHED: _____
_____
_____

WEATHER CONDITIONS: _____
_____
_____

WATER CONDITIONS: _____
_____
_____

FISH CAUGHT: _____
_____
_____

METHODS/COMMENTS: _____
_____
_____
_____
_____
_____
_____
_____

DATE: _____

LOCATION FISHED: _____

_____

_____

WEATHER CONDITIONS: _____

_____

_____

WATER CONDITIONS: _____

_____

_____

FISH CAUGHT: _____

_____

_____

METHODS/COMMENTS: _____

_____

_____

_____

_____

_____

_____

DATE: _____

LOCATION FISHED: _____
_____
_____

WEATHER CONDITIONS: _____
_____
_____

WATER CONDITIONS: _____
_____
_____

FISH CAUGHT: _____
_____
_____

METHODS/COMMENTS: _____
_____
_____
_____
_____
_____
_____
_____

DATE: _____

LOCATION FISHED: _____

_____

_____

WEATHER CONDITIONS: _____

_____

_____

WATER CONDITIONS: _____

_____

_____

FISH CAUGHT: _____

_____

_____

METHODS/COMMENTS: _____

_____

_____

_____

_____

_____

_____

_____

DATE: _____

LOCATION FISHED: _____
_____
_____

WEATHER CONDITIONS: _____
_____
_____

WATER CONDITIONS: _____
_____
_____

FISH CAUGHT: _____
_____
_____

METHODS/COMMENTS: _____
_____
_____
_____
_____
_____
_____
_____

DATE: _____

LOCATION FISHED: _____

_____

_____

WEATHER CONDITIONS: _____

_____

_____

WATER CONDITIONS: _____

_____

_____

FISH CAUGHT: _____

_____

_____

METHODS/COMMENTS: _____

_____

_____

_____

_____

_____

_____

DATE: _____

LOCATION FISHED: _____
_____
_____

WEATHER CONDITIONS: _____
_____
_____

WATER CONDITIONS: _____
_____
_____

FISH CAUGHT: _____
_____
_____

METHODS/COMMENTS: _____
_____
_____
_____
_____
_____
_____
_____

DATE: _____

LOCATION FISHED: _____
_____
_____

WEATHER CONDITIONS: _____
_____
_____

WATER CONDITIONS: _____
_____
_____

FISH CAUGHT: _____
_____
_____

METHODS/COMMENTS: _____
_____
_____
_____
_____
_____
_____
_____

DATE: _____

LOCATION FISHED: _____
_____
_____

WEATHER CONDITIONS: _____
_____
_____

WATER CONDITIONS: _____
_____
_____

FISH CAUGHT: _____
_____
_____

METHODS/COMMENTS: _____
_____
_____
_____
_____
_____
_____

Printed in Great Britain
by Amazon.co.uk, Ltd.,
Marston Gate.